The Colors We Eat

Green Foods

Patricia Whitehouse

Heinemann Library
Chicago, Illinois

© 2002 Reed Educational & Professional Publishing
Published by Heinemann Library,
an imprint of Reed Educational & Professional Publishing,
Chicago, Illinois

Customer Service 888-454-2279
Visit our website at www.heinemannlibrary.com

Designed by Sue Emerson, Heinemann Library
Printed and bound in the U.S.A. by Lake Book

06
10 9 8 7 6 5 4 3

Library of Congress Cataloging-in-Publication Data
Whitehouse, Patricia, 1958-
    Green foods / Patricia Whitehouse.
        p. cm. — (The colors we eat)
Includes index.
Summary: Introduces things to eat and drink that are green, from
honeydew melons to limeade.
    ISBN: 978-1-58810-535-6 (1-58810-535-0) (HC) ISBN: 978-1-58810-743-5 (1-58810-743-4) (Pbk)
    1. Food—Juvenile literature. 2. Green—Juvenile literature. [1.
    Food. 2. Green.] I. Title.
    TX355 .W46 2002
    641.3—dc21

                                        2001004795

Acknowledgments
The author and publishers are grateful to the following for permission to reproduce copyright material:
Title page, pp. 5, 6, 9, 16, 17, 18 Michael Brosilow/Heinemann Library; pp. 4, 8, 12, Dwight Kuhn; p. 7 Rob & Ann Simpson/Visuals Unlimited; p. 10 Rick Wetherbee; p. 11 E. R. Degginger; pp. 13, 15 David Siren/Visuals Unlimited; p. 14 John D. Cunningham/Visuals Unlimited; p. 19 Greg Beck/Fraser Photos; pp. 20L, 20R, 21 Craig Mitchelldyer Photography

Cover photograph by Michael Brosilow/Heinemann Library

Special thanks to our advisory panel for their help in the preparation of this book:
Eileen Day, Preschool Teacher
Chicago, IL

Paula Fischer, K–1 Teacher
Indianapolis, IN

Sandra Gilbert,
Library Media Specialist
Houston, TX

Angela Leeper,
Educational Consultant
North Carolina Department
of Public Instruction
Raleigh, NC

Pam McDonald, Reading Teacher
Winter Springs, FL

Melinda Murphy,
Library Media Specialist
Houston, TX

Helen Rosenberg, MLS
Chicago, IL

Anna Marie Varakin,
Reading Instructor
Western Maryland College

Some words are shown in bold, **like this.**
You can find them in the picture glossary on page 23.

Contents

Have You Eaten Green Foods?

Colors are all around you.

You might have eaten some of these colors.

There are green fruits
and vegetables.

There are other green foods, too.

What Are Some Big Green Foods?

Some melons are big and green.

Honeydew melons are light green.

Watermelons are big and green.

The hard green skin is called
the **rind.**

What Are Some Other Big Green Foods?

Some **cabbages** are big and green.

They grow close to the ground.

Lettuce heads are big and green.

People eat lettuce leaves in salads.

What Are Some Small Green Foods?

Some grapes are small and green.

They grow on **vines**.

Limes are small and green, too.

They grow on trees.

What Are Some Other Small Green Foods?

pod

seed

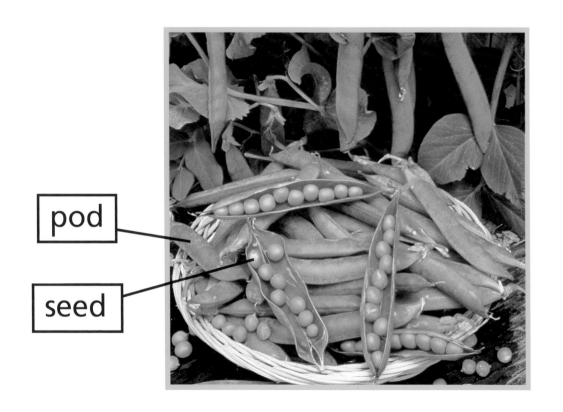

Peas are small and green.

Peas are seeds that grow inside **pods**.

Brussels sprouts are small and green, too.

They look like little lettuces.

What Are Some Crunchy Green Foods?

Celery is crunchy and green.

We eat the **stem** of the celery plant.

Broccoli is crunchy and green, too.

We eat the flowers of the broccoli plant.

What Are Some Soft Green Foods?

Kiwis are soft and green.

Sometimes people eat kiwis in salads

Avocados are soft and green, too.

Sometimes people eat mashed avocados.

What Green Foods Can You Drink?

Pea soup is green.

It is made by cooking peas.

Limeade is a green drink.

It is made by pressing the juice out of limes.

Green Salad Recipe

Ask an adult to help you.

First, wash some lettuce, celery, and cucumbers.

Next, cut them into small pieces.

Then, mix everything in a bowl.

Here's your green salad!

Quiz

Can you name these green foods?

Look for the answers on page 24.

Picture Glossary

avocado
page 17

pod
page 12

brussels sprouts
page 13

rind
page 7

cabbage
page 8

stem
page 14

honeydew melon
page 6

vine
page 10

kiwi
page 16

Note to Parents and Teachers

Reading for information is an important part of a child's literacy development. Learning begins with a question about something. Help children think of themselves as investigators and researchers by encouraging their questions about the world around them. Each chapter in this book begins with a question. Read the question together. Look at the pictures. Talk about what you think the answer might be. Then read the text to find out if your predictions were correct. Think of other questions you could ask about the topic, and discuss where you might find the answers. Assist children in using the picture glossary and the index to practice new vocabulary and research skills.

Index

Answers to quiz on page 22

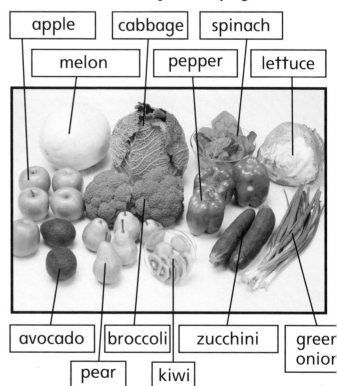

apple | cabbage | spinach | melon | pepper | lettuce | avocado | broccoli | zucchini | green onion | pear | kiwi